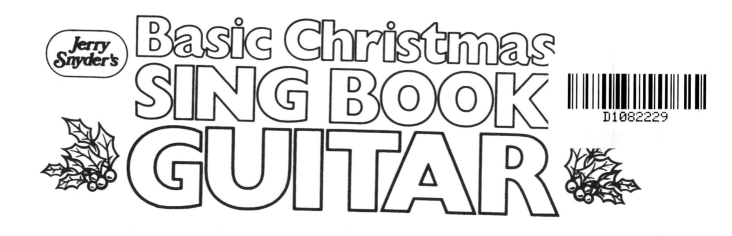

Jerry Snyder's Basic Christmas Sing Book Guitar

GUITAR STRUMS

A *strum* or *accompaniment* pattern is suggested for each of the songs in this book to add additional interest and to help set the mood of the song. The goal is to create your own original strums and to apply them in an individual manner.

EXPLANATION OF STRUM NOTATION

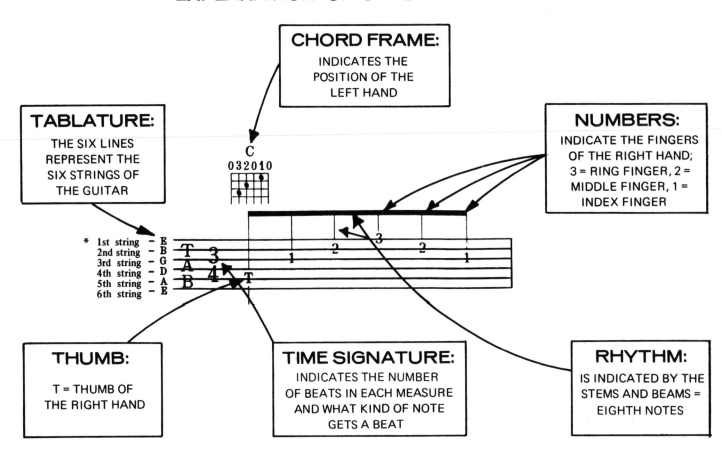

CHORD FRAME: INDICATES THE POSITION OF THE LEFT HAND

TABLATURE: THE SIX LINES REPRESENT THE SIX STRINGS OF THE GUITAR

NUMBERS: INDICATE THE FINGERS OF THE RIGHT HAND; 3 = RING FINGER, 2 = MIDDLE FINGER, 1 = INDEX FINGER

* 1st string — E
2nd string — B
3rd string — G
4th string — D
5th string — A
6th string — E

THUMB: T = THUMB OF THE RIGHT HAND

TIME SIGNATURE: INDICATES THE NUMBER OF BEATS IN EACH MEASURE AND WHAT KIND OF NOTE GETS A BEAT

RHYTHM: IS INDICATED BY THE STEMS AND BEAMS = EIGHTH NOTES

ACTUAL SOUND: THE STRUM DIAGRAMED ABOVE WOULD BE NOTATED IN STANDARD MUSIC NOTATION LIKE THIS — (NOTE: THE ACTUAL SOUND OF THE NOTE IS ONE OCTAVE LOWER THAN WRITTEN)

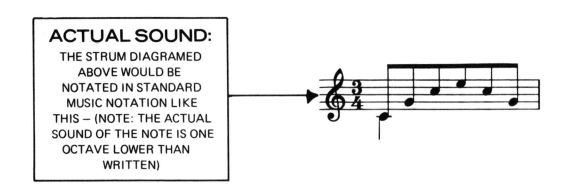

*NOTE: The 6th, 5th and 4th strings are called the **bass** strings. The 3rd, 2nd and 1st strings are the **treble** strings.

SYMBOL	REPRESENTS	TECHNIQUE
		BRUSH DOWN: STRUM WITH THE BACKS (NAILS) OF THE *INDEX* AND *MIDDLE* FINGERS DOWN ACROSS THE STRINGS (LOW TO HIGH).
		SWEEP DOWN: STRUM WITH THE *THUMB* DOWN ACROSS THE STRINGS (LOW TO HIGH).
		SCRATCH DOWN: STRUM WITH THE BACK (NAIL) OF THE *INDEX* FINGER DOWN ACROSS THE STRINGS (LOW TO HIGH). IN THIS EXAMPLE, ONLY THE TOP FOUR STRINGS ARE STRUMMED.
		SCRATCH UP: STRUM WITH THE FLESHY PART OF THE *INDEX* FINGER UPWARD ACROSS THE 1ST, 2ND AND 3RD STRINGS (HIGH TO LOW).
		3RD FINGER: PLUCK THE 1ST STRING (E) WITH THE *RING* FINGER OF THE RIGHT HAND.
		2ND FINGER: PLUCK THE 2ND STRING (B) WITH THE *MIDDLE* FINGER OF THE RIGHT HAND.
		1ST FINGER: PLUCK THE 3RD STRING (G) WITH THE *INDEX* FINGER OF THE RIGHT HAND.
		THUMB: PLUCK THE 5TH STRING (A) WITH THE RIGHT HAND *THUMB*.
		3RD AND 2ND FINGERS: *RING* AND *MIDDLE* FINGERS OF THE RIGHT HAND PLUCK THE 1ST (E) AND 2ND (B) STRINGS SIMULTANEOUSLY.
		MUTE: STRUM THE STRINGS DOWNWARD (LOW TO HIGH) WITH A *SCRATCH* STRUM AND IMMEDIATELY DAMPEN (SILENCE, DEADEN) THE STRINGS BY ROLLING ON TO THE HEEL OF THE HAND. USE ONE CONTINUOUS MOTION.

strum techniques

Various *strum techniques* such as the *BRUSH, SCRATCH, SWEEP* and *MUTE* may be combined to perform a variety of accompaniment patterns. To properly perform these techniques, the **RIGHT FOREARM** should rest on the edge of the guitar approximately above the bridge bass or asddle. The fingers are slightly *curved* and *bunched* together with the **THUMB EXTENDED** toward the sound hole of the guitar.

Arm and Hand Position

1. Place the *forearm* on the lower bout of the guitar above the bridge base.
2. Two adjustments can be made for varying differences in the size of arms and guitars;
   a. adjust along the forearm; that is, forward or backward.
   b. adjust along the bout of the guitar; that is, to the left or right.
3. The arm should feel **BALANCED**.
4. Now rotate the **WRIST** to bring the **HAND** into position. The **FINGERS** should be at right angles to the strings.

brush

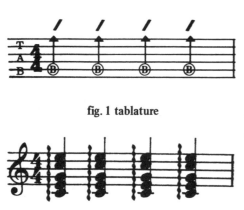

fig. 1 tablature

fig. 2 standard notation

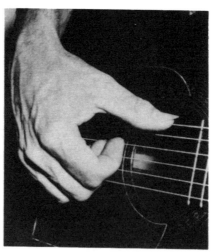

Preparation

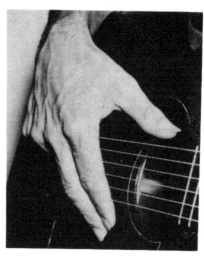

Completion

BRUSH down across the strings (bass to treble) with the nails of the *index* and *middle* fingers. Keep the fingers bunched together. The **PRIMARY** motion of the strum is *finger* motion. With the fingers slightly curled above the strings, simply "open up" the hand allowing the fingers to brush the strings.

For additional power and emphasis a **SECONDARY** motion can be added. As you *brush* down across the strings, add a "flick" of the wrist.

sweep

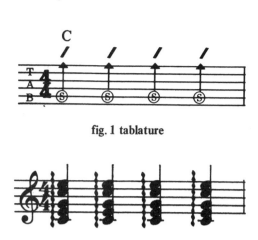

fig. 1 tablature

Preparation

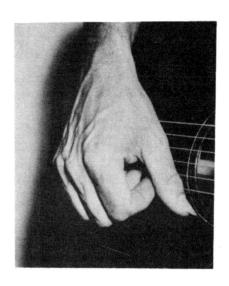

Completion

fig. 2 standard notation

SWEEP downward across the strings (bass to treble) with the ***thumb***. The thumb should be kept straight and rigid. The sound is produced by a combination of flesh and nail (depending on the length of your nail). The **PRIMARY** motion is in the wrist. The **SECONDARY** motion is in the thumb as it moves toward the fingers. **DO NOT** bend the thumb at the first joint.

scratch—down

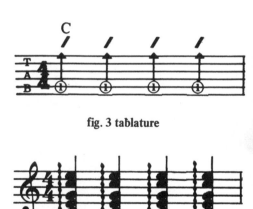

fig. 3 tablature

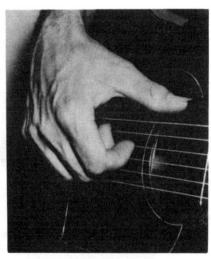

Preparation

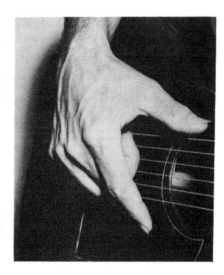

Completion

fig. 4 standard notation

SCRATCH down across the strings (bass to treble) with the nail of the ***index*** finger. The **PRIMARY** motion of the strum is finger motion. Attempt to keep the hand above the strings.

For additional emphasis and power, add some *wrist* motion to the scratch. As you scratch downward, give a slight "flick" of the wrist.

scratch—up

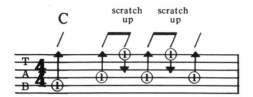

fig. 1 tablature

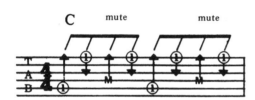

fig. 2 standard notation

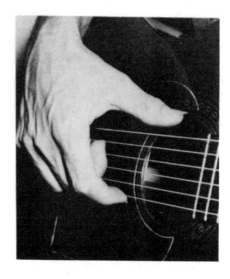

Preparation

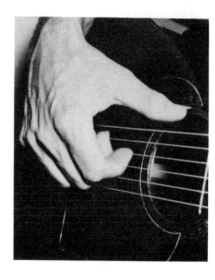

Completion

SCRATCH upward across the treble strings with the fleshy part of the *index* finger. It is only necessary to strum the 1st, 2nd and 3rd strings. The upward scratch is most often performed in alternation with the downward scratch; that is, scratch down-up-down-up, etc. The **PRIMARY** motion of the strum is a finger motion with just a slight inward turning of the wrist. When performing the scratch, keep the hand above the strings and use a minimum of motion.

mute

fig. 3 tablature

fig. 4 standard notation

Preparation

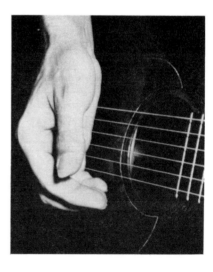

Completion

Scratch down across the strings (bass to treble) and immediately *MUTE* or dampen (silence) the strings by rolling on to the strings with the *side* or *heel* of the hand. This should be done in *one continuous motion* downward. The **PRIMARY** motion of the mute is in the wrist as you turn the hand and roll on to its side.

finger techniques

The *THUMB* and *FINGERS* are used to play *plucks, arpeggios, pulls, pinches* and *finger-picking* patterns. The basic technique used is called a **FREE STROKE** *(tirando)*. The *THUMB* should be kept straight and rigid and should extend toward the soundhole. The *FINGERS* should be slightly curved and bunched together.

FINGERS

Place the **index** finger on the *3rd string*, the **middle** finger on the *2nd string*, the **ring** finger on the *1st string* and the **thumb** on the *6th string*. The *FINGERS* are bunched together and slightly arched. Now *squeeze* until you have *pushed* the fingers passed the strings. The fingers should pass over the adjacent (neighboring) strings. The **PRIMARY** motion of the **FREE STROKE** is at the *knuckle*. There is a **SECONDARY** motion in the second joint. Do not collapse the first joint of the fingers.

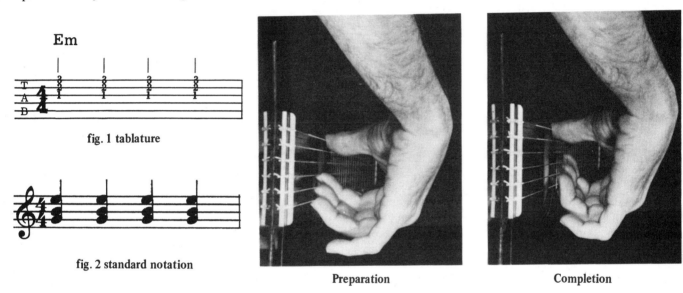

Em

fig. 1 tablature

fig. 2 standard notation

Preparation

Completion

THUMB

Push the string with the **THUMB** toward the adjacent (neighboring) string. At the completion of the **FREE STROKE**, the *thumb* passes over and slightly above the adjacent string. The **PRIMARY** motion is from the *knuckle* or second joint of the thumb. Keep the thumb rigid and **DO NOT** bend or collapse the first joint.

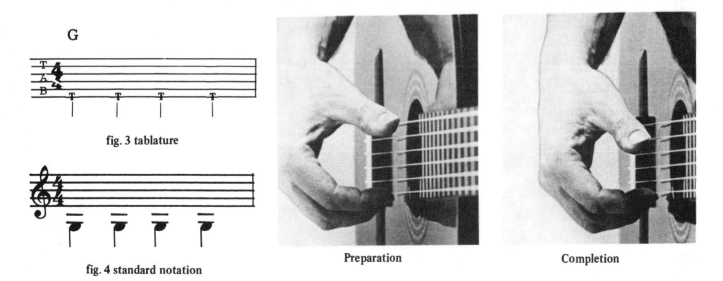

G

fig. 3 tablature

fig. 4 standard notation

Preparation

Completion

Have Yourself A Merry Little Christmas

From The Videocraft Musical Spectacular "RUDOLPH THE RED-NOSED REINDEER"

Rudolph, The Red-Nosed Reindeer

Words and Music by
JOHNNY MARKS

CHORDS USED IN THIS SONG:

SUGGESTED STRUM:

Count: 1 da 2 da 3 da 4 da

Plucking/Arpeggio pattern: thumb plucks the root (R) of the chord; fingers pluck the treble strings; optional - alternate to the fifth (5) on 3.

You know Dash-er and Dan-cer and Pran-cer and Vix-en, Com-et and Cu-pid and Don-ner and Blitz-en, but do you re-call the most fa-mous rein-deer of all?

Chorus:

1. Ru-dolph the red-nosed rein-deer had a ver-y shin-y nose
2. All of the oth-er rein-deer used to laugh and call him names
3. Then how the rein-deer loved him as they shout-ed out with glee:

And if you ev-er saw it, you would e-ven say it glows.
They nev-er let poor Ru-dolf join in an-y rein-deer games.
"Ru-dolph, the red-nosed rein-deer, you'll go down in his-to-

1.
2. *To next strain*

3. *Fine*
ry." Then one fog-gy Christ-mas Eve, San-ta came to say:

D.S. al fine
"Ru-dolph with your nose so bright, won't you guide my sleigh to-night."

WINTER WONDERLAND

Words by
DICK SMITH

Music by
FELIX BERNARD

Sleigh-bells ring; are you lis - t'nin'? In the lane snow is glis - t'nin'. A beau - ti - ful sight, __ we're hap - py to - night, __ walk - in' in a win - ter won - der - land! Gone a - way is the blue - bird. Here to stay is a new bird. { He He's sings a love song __ } { sing - in' a song __ } as we go a - long, __ walk - ing in a win - ter won - der -

I Saw Mommy Kissing Santa Claus

Words and Music by
TOMMIE CONNOR

The Little Drummer Boy

Words and Music by KATHERINE DAVIS,
HENRY ONARATI and HARRY SIMEONE

Santa Claus Is Coming To Town

Words by HAVEN GILLESPIE
Music by J. FRED COOTS

SUGGESTED STRUM:

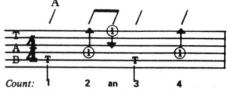

Count: 1   2 an 3   4

Thumb/Scratch variation: thumb plucks the root (R) of the chord; optional - thumb plucks the fifth (5) of the chord on 3.

CHORDS USED IN THIS SONG:

Moderately

1. You bet-ter watch out, you bet-ter not cry, Bet-ter not pout, I'm
2. mak-ing a list and check-ing it twice, Gon-na find out who's
3. bet-ter watch out, you bet-ter not cry, Bet-ter not pout, I'm

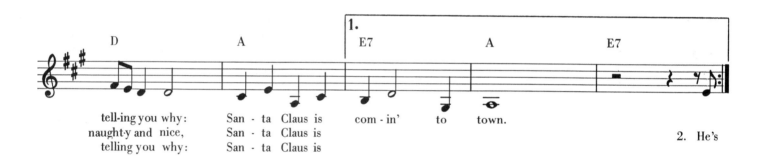

tell-ing you why: San-ta Claus is com-in' to town.
naught-y and nice, San-ta Claus is
telling you why: San-ta Claus is

2. He's

com-in' to town. _____ He com-in' to town. _____

sees you when you're sleep-in', He knows why you're a-wake, He

knows if you've been bad or good, so be good for good-ness sake. 3. Oh! You

Here Comes Santa Claus
(Right Down Santa Claus Lane)

Words and Music by
GENE AUTRY and OAKLEY HALDEMAN

Angels We Have Heard On High

TRADITIONAL

Deck The Halls

TRADITIONAL

Good King Wenceslas

TRADITIONAL

CHORDS USED IN THIS SONG:

SUGGESTED STRUM:

Count: 1   2   an   3   4

Brush/Scratch variation: give emphasis to the first beat of the measure.

Moderately

1.Good King Wen - ces - las looked out   on the feast of
2."Hith - er, page, and stand by me,   if thou know'st it,

Steph - en,   when the snow lay 'round a - bout,
tell - ing,   yon - der peas - ant, who is he,

deep and crisp and e - ven;   bright - ly shone the
where and what is dwell - ing?"   "Sire, he lives a

moon and night,   through the frost was cru - el,   when a poor man
good league hence   un - der - neath the moun - tain;   right a - gainst the

came in sight,   gath -'ring win - ter fu - el.
for - est fence,   by Saint Ag - nes foun - tain."

It Came Upon The Midnight Clear

Words and Music by
Rev. E. H. SEARS
and R. S. WILLIS

CHORDS USED IN THIS SONG:

SUGGESTED STRUM:

Joy To The World

Words by ISAAC WATTS
Music by G. F. HANDEL

O Little Town Of Bethlehem

Words and Music by
PHILLIP BROOKS
and L. H. REDNER

Silent Night

Words and Music by
JOSEPH MOHR and
FRANZ GRUBER

Up On The House-Top

TRADITIONAL

SUGGESTED STRUM:

CHORDS USED IN THIS SONG:

Count: **1** an **2** an **3** an **4** an

Thumb/Finger strum: sweep downward across the strings; scratch an up-down pattern.

Brightly

Verse:

1. Up on the house - top ___ rein - deer pause.
2. First comes the stock - ing of lit - tle Nell;
3. Next comes the stock - ing of lit - tle Will:

Out jumps good old San - ta Claus. Down thro' the chim - ny with
Oh, dear San - ta fill it well: Give her a dol - ly that
Oh, just see what a glo - rious fill! Here is a ham - mer and

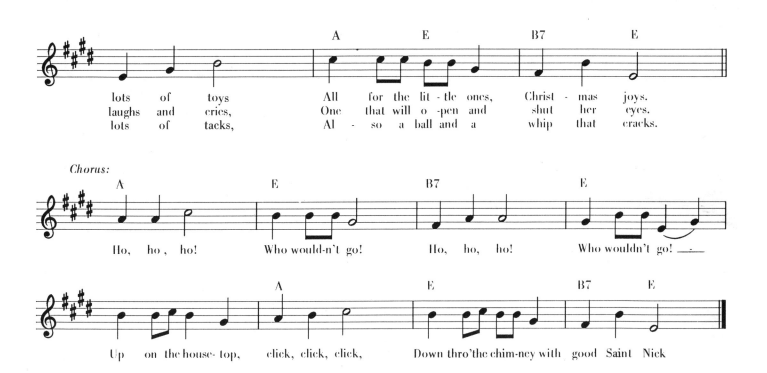

lots of toys All for the lit - tle ones, Christ - mas joys.
laughs and cries, One that will o - pen and shut her eyes.
lots of tacks, Al - so a ball and a whip that cracks.

Chorus:

Ho, ho, ho! Who would-n't go! Ho, ho, ho! Who wouldn't go! ___

Up on the house- top, click, click, click, Down thro'the chim-ney with good Saint Nick

What Child Is This?

By WILLIAM C. DIX
Based on "Greensleeves"

From The Videocraft Musical Spectacular "RUDOLPH THE RED-NOSED REINDEER"

Silver And Gold

Words and Music by
JOHNNY MARKS

O Christmas Tree

TRADITIONAL GERMAN CAROL

CHORDS USED IN THIS SONG:

SUGGESTED STRUM:

Count: 1 2 3

Sweep/Brush strum: thumb sweeps downward on 1; fingers brush downward on 2 and 3; or, use a flat-pick.

Slowly

1. O Christ - mas tree O Christ - mas tree, how beau - ti - ful and
2. O Christ - mas tree O Christ - mas tree, your branch- es green de -
3. O Christ - mas tree O Christ - mas tree, you give us so much

bright, _____ O Christ - mas tree, O Christ - mas tree, how
light us. O Christ - mas tree. O Christ - mas tree, you
plea - sure! O Christ - mas tree, O Christ - mas tree, you

beau - ti - ful and bright. _____ The sight of thee at
branch- es green de - light us. They're green when sum - mer
give us so much plea - sure! How oft at Christ - mas -

Christ-mas tide, spreads hope and glad - ness far and wide. O
days and bright; they're green when win - ter snow and white. O
tide the sight, O green fir tree, gives us de - light. O

Christ - mas tree, O Christ - mas tree, how beau - ti - ful and bright. ____
Christ - mas tree, O Christ - mas tree, your branch- es green de - light us.
Christ - mas tree, O Christ - mas tree, you give us so much plea - sure!

From The Videocraft T.V. Music Spectacular "RUDOLPH THE RED-NOSED REINDEER

Jingle, Jingle, Jingle

By
JOHNNY MARKS

From The Videocraft T.V. Musical Spectacular "RUDOLPH THE RED-NOSED REINDEER"

A Holly Jolly Christmas

By JOHNNY MARKS

The First Noel

TRADITIONAL

Christmas Eve In My Home Town

Words and Music by
STAN ZABKA and DON UPTON

Christmas Eve In My Home Town - 2 - 1

From The Videocraft Musical Spectacular "RUDOLPH THE RED-NOSED REINDEER"

The Night Before Christmas Song

From Clement Moore's Poem
Lyric adapted by JOHNNY MARKS
Music by JOHNNY MARKS

CHORDS USED IN THIS SONG:

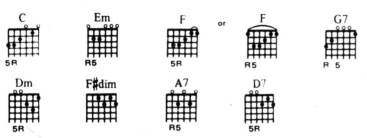

SUGGESTED STRUM:

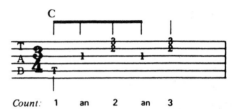

Count: 1 an 2 an 3
Thumb/Arpeggio pattern: thumb plucks the root
(R) of the chord; fingers pluck the treble strings.

Note: Chords in parenthesis may be omitted

Briskly

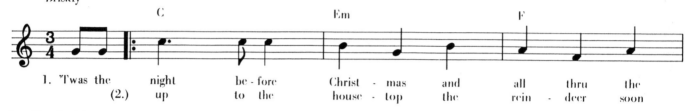

1. 'Twas the night be-fore Christ-mas and all thru the
(2.) up to the house-top and the rein-deer soon

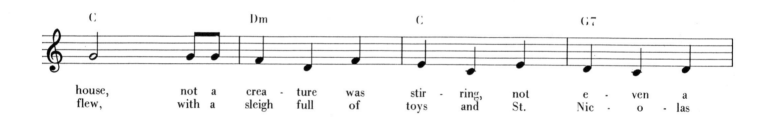

house, not a crea-ture was stir-ring, not e-ven a
flew, with a sleigh full of toys and St. Nic-o-las

mouse. All the stock-ings were hung by the chim-ney with
too. Down the chim-ney he came with a leap and a

care, In the hope that St. Nich-o-las soon would be
bound, He was dressed all in fur and his bel-ly was

there. The what to my won-der-ing eyes should ap-
round. He spoke not a word but went straight to his

The Night Before Christmas Song - 2 - 1

Away In The Manger

Words and Music by
J. E. SPILLMAN
and MARTIN LUTHER

SUGGESTED STRUM:

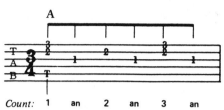

Count: 1 an 2 an 3 an

Plucking/Arpeggio variation: thumb plucks the root (R) of the chord; fingers pluck the treble strings in broken chord fashion.

CHORDS USED IN THIS SONG:

Moderately

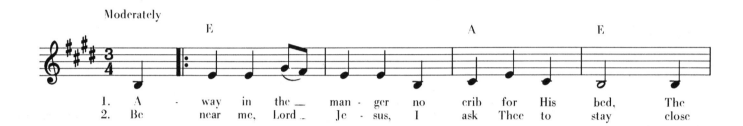

1. A — way in the __ man - ger no crib for His bed, The
2. Be near me, Lord __ Je - sus, I ask Thee to stay close

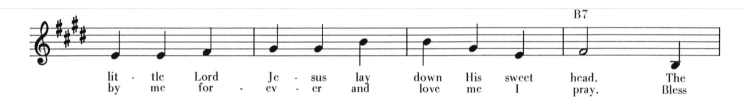

lit - tle Lord Je - sus lay down His sweet head. The
by me for - ev - er and love me I pray. The Bless

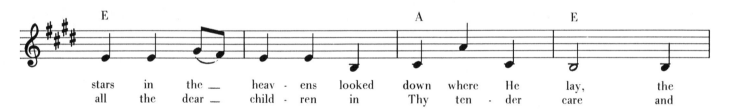

stars in the __ heav - ens looked down where He lay, the
all the dear __ child - ren in Thy ten - der care and

lit - tle Lord Je - sus a - sleep in the hay. The __
take us to Heav - en to live with Thee there. A -

cat - tle are low - ing the poor ba - by wakes. But __
way in a man - ger, no crib for His bed, The __

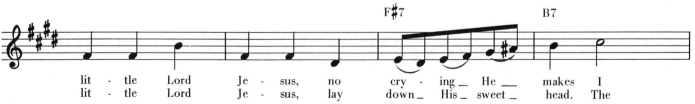

lit - tle Lord Je - sus, no cry - ing __ He __ makes I
lit - tle Lord Je - sus, lay down __ His __ sweet __ head. The

Away In The Manger - 2 - 1

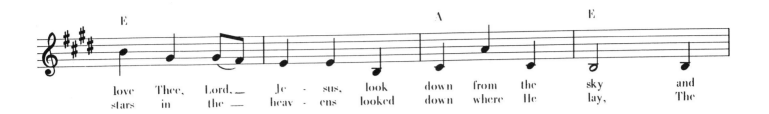

love Thee, Lord,— Je - sus, look down from the sky, and
stars in the — heav - ens looked down down where He lay,

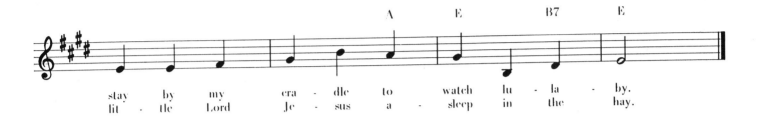

stay by my cra - dle to watch lu - la - by.
lit - tle Lord Je - sus a - sleep in the hay.

I Saw Three Ships

TRADITIONAL

CHORDS USED IN THIS SONG:

G   C   D

SUGGESTED STRUM:

Count: 1 —— 2 3

Pull/Brush variation: fingers and thumb pluck or pull the treble strings and root (R) of the chord; brush down with the fingers on 3.

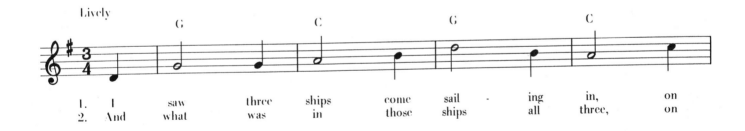

Lively   G   C   G   C

1. I saw three ships come sail - ing in, on
2. And saw what was in those ships all three, on

G   D   G   C

Christ - mas Day, On Christ - mas Day; I saw three ships come those
Christ - mas Day, On Christ - mas Day; And saw what was in those

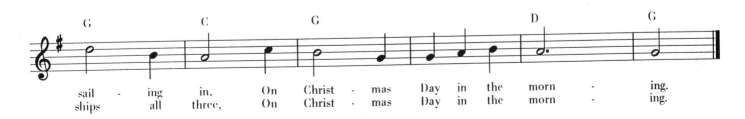

G   C   G   D   G

sail - ing in, On Christ - mas Day in the morn - ing.
ships all three, On Christ - mas Day in the morn - ing.

The Holly And The Ivy

TRADITIONAL

SUGGESTED STRUM:

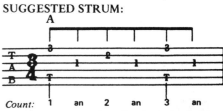

Count: 1 an 2 an 3 an

Pinch/Arpeggio variation: thumb plucks the root (R) of the chord; optional - thumb plucks the fifth (5) of the chord on 3.

CHORDS USED IN THIS SONG:

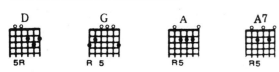

D   G   A   A7

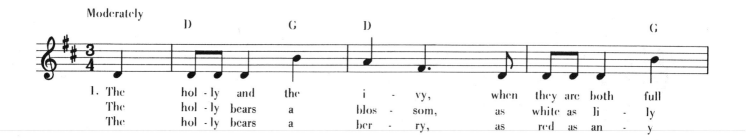

1. The hol-ly and the i - vy, when they are both full
   The hol-ly bears a blos - som, as white as li - ly
   The hol-ly bears a ber - ry, as red as an - y

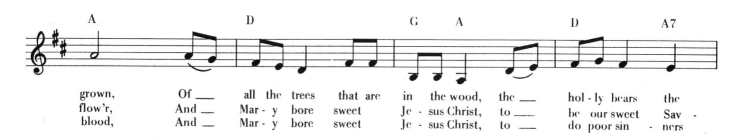

grown,   Of __ all the trees that are in the wood, the __ hol-ly bears the
flow'r,   And __ Mar-y bore sweet Je - sus Christ, to __ be our sweet Sav -
blood,   And __ Mar-y bore sweet Je - sus Christ, to __ do poor sin - ners

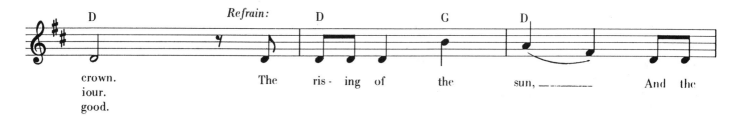

crown.   The ris - ing of the sun, _____ And the
iour.
good.

run - ning of the deer,   the ____ play - ing of the

mer - ry or - gan, sweet sing - ing in the choir.

The Coventry Carol

TRADITIONAL ENGLISH

Sleigh Ride

Lyric by MITCHELL PARISH
Music by LEROY ANDERSON

CHORDS USED IN THIS SONG:

SUGGESTED STRUM:

Count: 1 2 3 4

Thumb/Brush variation: thumb plucks the root (R) of the chord; fingers brush down across the strings; optional - thumb plucks fifth (5) on 3.

Moderately bright

Just hear those sleigh bells jin-gle-ing, ring-ting-tin-gle-ing, too, _____ Come on it's love-ly weath-er for a Sleigh Ride to-geth-er with you. _____ Out-side the snow is fall-ing and friends are call-ing "Yoo hoo", _____ Come on, it's love-ly weath-er for a Sleigh Ride to-geth-er with you. _____ Gid-dy-yap, gid-dy yap, gid-dy yap, let's go, Let's look at the snow We're rid-ing in a

Sleigh Ride - 2 - 1

The Twelve Days Of Christmas

TRADITIONAL

The Twelve Days Of Christmas - 2 - 1

The Twelve Days Of Christmas - 2 - 2

Thirty-Two Feet And Eight Little Tails

Words and Music by JOHN REDMOND
JAMES CAVANAUGH and FRANK WELDON

SUGGESTED STRUM:

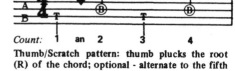

Count: 1 an 2 3 4

Thumb/Scratch pattern: thumb plucks the root (R) of the chord; optional - alternate to the fifth (5) on 3.

CHORDS USED IN THIS SONG:

NOTE: Chords in parenthesis may be omitted

Moderately bright

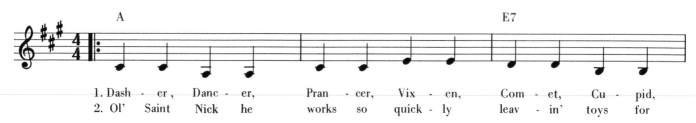

1. Dash - er, Danc - er, Pran - cer, Vix - en, Com - et, Cu - pid,
2. Ol' Saint Nick he works so quick - ly leav - in' toys for

Don - ner, Blitz - en O - ver the moon so bright
girls and boys. Then o - ver the roof so high

Thir - ty two feet and eight lit - tle tails of white, _____
Thir - ty two feet and eight lit - tle tails they fly. _____

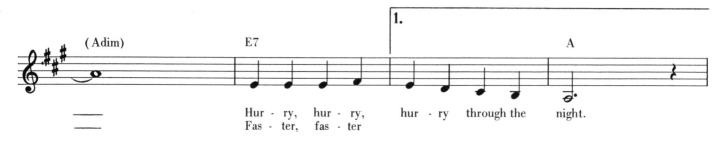

Hur - ry, hur - ry, hur - ry through the night.
Fas - ter, fas - ter

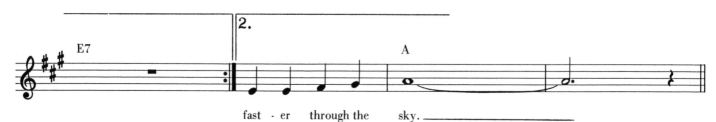

fast - er through the sky. _____

Thirty-Two Feet And Eight Little Tails - 2 - 1

Ohhh! _____ Look at 'em go, _____

San - ta laugh - in' Ho, ho, ho, ho, ho, ho, ho, ho, ho,

Dash - er, Dan - cer, Pran - cer, Vix - en, Com - et, Cu - pid,

Don - ner, Blitz - en, o - ver the gar - den wall,

Thir - ty -two feet and eight lit - tle tails an' all, _____

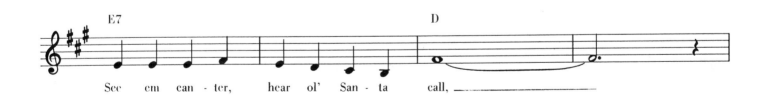

See em can - ter, hear ol' San - ta call, _____

"Mer - ry mer - ry Christ - mas to you all." _____

Thirty-Two Feet And Eight Little Tails - 2 - 2

Hark! The Herald Angels Sing

Words and Music by
FELIX MENDELSSOHN
and CHAS. WESLEY

CHORDS USED IN THIS SONG:

SUGGESTED STRUM:

Count: 1 2 3 4

Pull/Pluck pattern; fingers pull or pluck the treble
strings; thumb plucks the root (R) of the chord.

NOTE : Chords in parenthesis may be omitted

1. Hark the her - ald an - gels sing, ___ "Glo - ry to the
2. Christ by high - est heav'n a - dored, ___ Christ the ev - er

new born King! Peace on earth and mer - cy mild, ___
last - ing Lord. Late in time be - hold him come, ___

God and sin - ners re - con - ciled." Joy - ful all ye
Off - spring of the Vir - gin's womb. Veiled in flesh the

na - tions rise, ___ Join the tri - umph of the skies; ___ With an - gel - ic
God - head see, ___ Hail th'in car - nate De - i - ty. ___ Pleased as man with

host pro - claim, "Christ is ___ born in Beth - le - hem."
men ap - pear, Je - sus, ___ our Em - man - u - el.

Hark! the her - ald an - gels sing, "Glo - ry ___ to the new born King!
Hark! the her - ald an - gels sing, "Glo - ry ___ to the new born King!

Jingle Bells

Words and Music by
J. PIERPONT

Rockin' Around The Christmas Tree

Words and Music by
JOHNNY MARKS

CHORDS USED IN THIS SONG:

SUGGESTED STRUM:

Count: 1   2 an - 3 an 4

Syncopated strum: give emphasis to the accented beat - 2 an.

Moderate

Rock-in a -round the Christ-mas-tree_ at the Christ-mas par-ty hop. ___
Rock-in a -round the Christ-mas-tree_ let the Christ-mas spir-it ring. ___

Mis-tle-toe hung where you can see ev-'ry cou-ple tries to stop.
Lat-er we'll have some pun-kin-pie and we'll do some car-ol-

ing. You will get a sent-i-men-tal feel-ing when you hear

voic-es sing-ing, "Let's be jol-ly, Deck the halls with boughs of hol-ly."

Rock-in a -round the Christ-mas tree._ Have a hap-py hol-i-day. ___

Ev-'ry-one danc-ing mer-ri-ly ___ in the new old fash-ioned way.

O Come, All Ye Faithful

Trans. by F. OAKLEY
By WARDS "CANTUS DIVERSI"

We Three Kings Of Orient Are

Words and Music by
Rev. J. H. HOPKINS

CHORDS USED IN THIS SONG:

SUGGESTED STRUM:

Patapan

Words and Music by
EUGENE MITCHELL
Burgundian Carol

SUGGESTED STRUM:

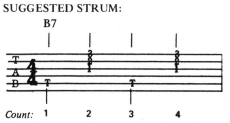

Count: 1 2 3 4

Thumb/Pluck: thumb plucks the root (R) of the chord; fingers pluck the treble strings; optional - thumb plucks the fifth (5) of the chord on 3.

CHORDS USED IN THIS SONG:

 Em B7 Am

Briskly

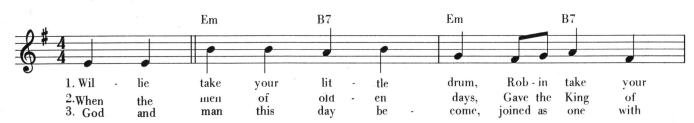

1. Wil - lie take your lit - tle drum, Rob - in take your
2. When the men of old - en days, Gave the King of
3. God and man this day be - come, joined as one with

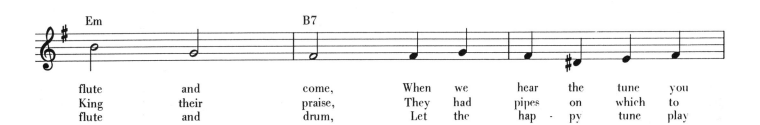

flute and come, When we hear the tune you
King their praise, They had pipes on which to
flute and drum, Let the hap - py tune play

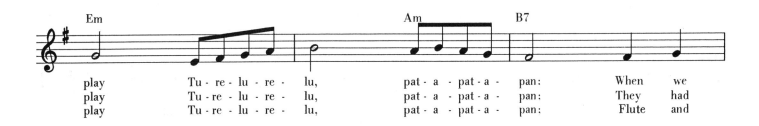

play Tu - re - lu - re - lu, pat - a - pat - a - pan: When we
play Tu - re - lu - re - lu, pat - a - pat - a - pan: They had
play Tu - re - lu - re - lu, pat - a - pat - a - pan: Flute and

hear the tune you play, How can an - y - one be glum?
drums on which to play. Full of joy on ___ Christ - mas Day.
drum to - geth - er play. As we sing on ___ Christ - mas Day.

God Rest Ye Merry, Gentlemen

TRADITIONAL

Jolly Old Saint Nicholas

TRADITIONAL

Masters In This Hall

TRADITIONAL

SUGGESTED STRUM:

CHORDS USED IN THIS SONG:

Count: 1 - 2   3   4 - 5   6

Thumb/Brush variation: thumb plucks the root (R) of the chord; fingers brush down across the strings; optional - thumb plucks the fifth (5) on 3.

With spirit

1. Mas - ters in this hall, _____ . Hear ye news to - day, _____
2. Go - ing o'er the hills, Thro' the milk white snow. _

Brought from o - ver sea, And ev - er I you pray.
Heard I ewes bleat while the wind did blow.

No - well! No - well! No - well! No - well sing we clear! Hol - pen

are all folk on earth __ Born __ is God's son so dear

No - well! No - well! No - well! No - well sing we loud! God to -

day hath poor folk raised, __ and __ cast a - down the proud.

I'll Be Home For Christmas

Words and Music by
KIM GANNON and WALTER KENT

CHORDS USED IN THIS SONG:

SUGGESTED STRUM:

I Heard The Bells On Christmas Day

Words by
HENRY WADSWORTH LONGFELLOW
Music by **JOHN MARKS**

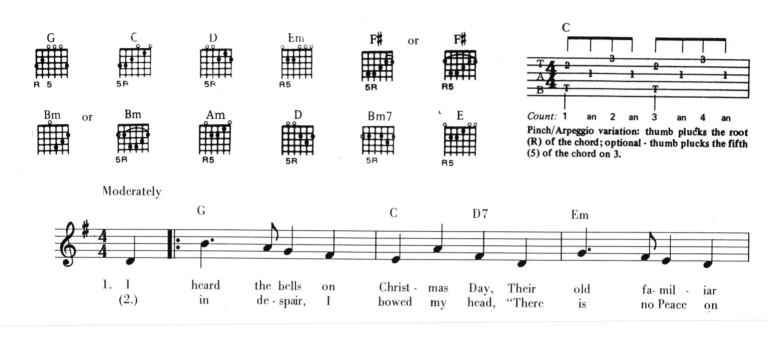

Count: 1 an 2 an 3 an 4 an

Pinch/Arpeggio variation: thumb plucks the root (R) of the chord; optional - thumb plucks the fifth (5) of the chord on 3.

Moderately

1. I heard the bells on Christ-mas Day, Their old fa-mil-iar
(2.) in de-spair, I bowed my head, "There is no Peace on

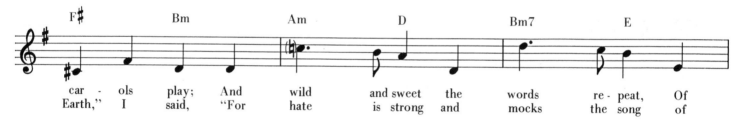

car-ols play; And wild and sweet the words re-peat, Of
Earth," I said, "For wild hate is strong and mocks the song of

Peace On Earth, Good Will to Men. I thought, as now this
Peace On Earth, Good Will to Men." Then pealed the bells more

day has come, The bel-fries of all Chris-ten-dom had rung so long the un-
loud and deep, "God is not dead, nor doth He sleep, the wrong shall fail, the

bro-ken song, of Peace On Earth, Good Will to Men. 2. And
right pre-vail, With Peace On Earth, Good Will to Men.

Stand Beneath The Mistletoe

Words and Music by
LOUIS HOLLINGSWORTH

From "BABES IN TOYLAND"

Toyland

Words by GLEN MAC DONOUGH
Music by VICTOR HERBERT

land   your   child - hood   knew! _____   Your   child -   hood

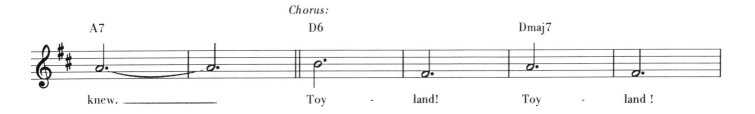

Chorus:

knew. _____   Toy -   land!   Toy -   land !

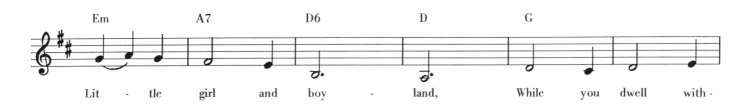

Lit -   tle   girl   and   boy -   land,   While   you   dwell   with -

in   it _____   You   are   ev -   er   hap -   py   then. _____

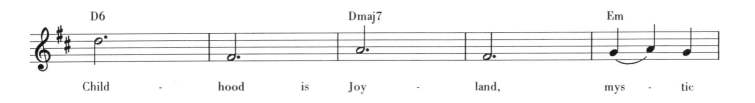

Child -   hood   is   Joy -   land,   mys -   tic

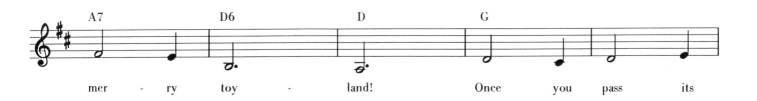

mer -   ry   toy -   land!   Once   you   pass   its

bor - ders   you   can   ne'er - re -   turn   a - gain. _____

Toyland - 2 - 2

When Santa Claus Gets Your Letter

Words and Music by
JOHNNY MARKS

There Is No Christmas Like A Home Christmas